What does it mean to have

Down's syndrome

Louise Spilsbury

Heinemann
LIBRARY

H www.heinemann.co.uk/library
Visit our website to find out more information about Heinemann Library books.

To order:
☎ Phone 44 (0) 1865 888066
▤ Send a fax to 44 (0) 1865 314091
▢ Visit the Heinemann Bookshop at www.heinemann.co.uk/library to browse our catalogue and order online.

First published in Great Britain by Heinemann Library,
Halley Court, Jordan Hill, Oxford OX2 8EJ,
a division of Reed Educational and Professional Publishing Ltd.
Heinemann is a registered trademark of Reed Educational and Professional Publishing Ltd.

OXFORD MELBOURNE AUCKLAND
JOHANNESBURG BLANTYRE GABORONE
IBADAN PORTSMOUTH (NH) USA CHICAGO

Designed by AMR
Originated by Dot Gradations
Printed in China by Wing King Tong

ISBN 0 431 13935 0 (hardback)   ISBN 0 431 13942 3 (paperback)
06 05 04 03 02   08 07 06 05 04 03
10 9 8 7 6 5 4 3 2 1   10 9 8 7 6 5 4 3 2 1

British Library Cataloguing in Publication Data
Spilsbury, Louise
   What does it mean to have Downs syndrome?
   1.Down syndrome – Juvenile literature
   I.Title II.Down's syndrome
   616.8'58842

Acknowledgements
The publishers would like to thank the following for permission to reproduce photographs: Corbis/Laura Dwight: pp.4, 8; Corbis/Lester B Bergman: p.5; Sally and Richard Greenhill: pp.7, 16, 17, 18, 19, 23, 24, 26; Down's Syndrome Association: p.14; Medipics: p.11; Chris Schwarz: pp.12, 13, 20, 21, 28, 29; Science Photo Library/Kevin Beebe/Custom Medical Stock Photo: p.9; Science Photo Library/CNRI: p.6; Science Photo Library/Richard Hutchings: p.15; Science Photo Library/Elaine Rebman: p.25; Science Photo Library/Hattie Young: pp.10, 22, 27.

Special thanks to: Karen and Kieran, Becky and Katherine.

The publishers would also like to thank: the Down's Syndrome Association, and Julie Johnson, PHSE Consultant Trainer and Writer, for their help in the preparation of this book.

Cover photograph reproduced with permission of Chris Schwartz.

Every effort has been made to contact copyright holders of any material reproduced in this book. Any omissions will be rectified in subsequent printings if notice is given to the publishers.

Contents

Any words appearing in the text in bold, **like this**, are explained in the Glossary.

What is Down's syndrome?

Down's syndrome is a **condition** that some people are born with. Most babies who are born with Down's syndrome have it because they have an extra **chromosome** in each of the **cells** in their body. Chromosomes carry **genes**, which are the things that control the way our bodies grow and develop.

Just as each one of us is different, each person who has Down's syndrome is different, but the condition always affects the way a person develops and learns in some way. People with Down's syndrome usually have some **learning difficulties**. This means they have trouble learning and remembering things in the same way as other people. For example, they usually take longer to learn how to walk and talk when they are little.

Just like anyone else, people with Down's syndrome have a wide range of hobbies and interests, from reading books to riding bicycles.

Each person who has Down's syndrome is different, and Down's syndrome is certainly not the most important thing about them. It is just a small part of who they are.

Different people who have Down's syndrome have different kinds of difficulties. Most children with Down's syndrome read and write, and go to ordinary schools. When they grow up, they look after themselves and get jobs to earn their living.

Why is it called 'Down's syndrome?'

Down's syndrome is named after an English doctor called John Langdon Down. In 1866, he became the first person to write a full description of what Down's syndrome is like. The word 'syndrome' simply means a set of signs or **symptoms** that go with a particular condition.

Although J L Down wrote about Down's syndrome, he did not know what caused it. It was not until 1959 that a French scientist, Jérôme Lejeune, discovered that Down's syndrome is caused by an extra chromosome.

How do chromosomes work?

Chromosomes play a vital part in everyone's lives. Chromosomes are tiny threads that are found inside every **cell** in your body. They carry the instructions that tell cells how to live, grow and work. These instructions are called **genes**. The kinds of genes we have determines the way we look – whether we have black or brown hair, blue or green eyes, or whether we grow tall or short.

There are usually 46 chromosomes in your cells. These are arranged in pairs – 23 sets of two – and numbered 1 to 23. A baby starts to grow inside its mother when two special cells – a **sperm** cell from the father and an **ovum** (egg cell) from the mother – come together. Each of the parent cells contains 23 chromosomes, so when they come together they make a complete set of 46.

What are cells?

Our bodies are made up of millions of tiny living parts called cells. These are so small you can only see them through a microscope. Different types of cells carry out different kinds of jobs, but they all contain chromosomes.

In each human body cell there are usually 23 pairs of chromosomes. One of each pair comes from the mother, the other from the father. One pair is different – this is the pair that determines whether a baby is a boy or a girl.

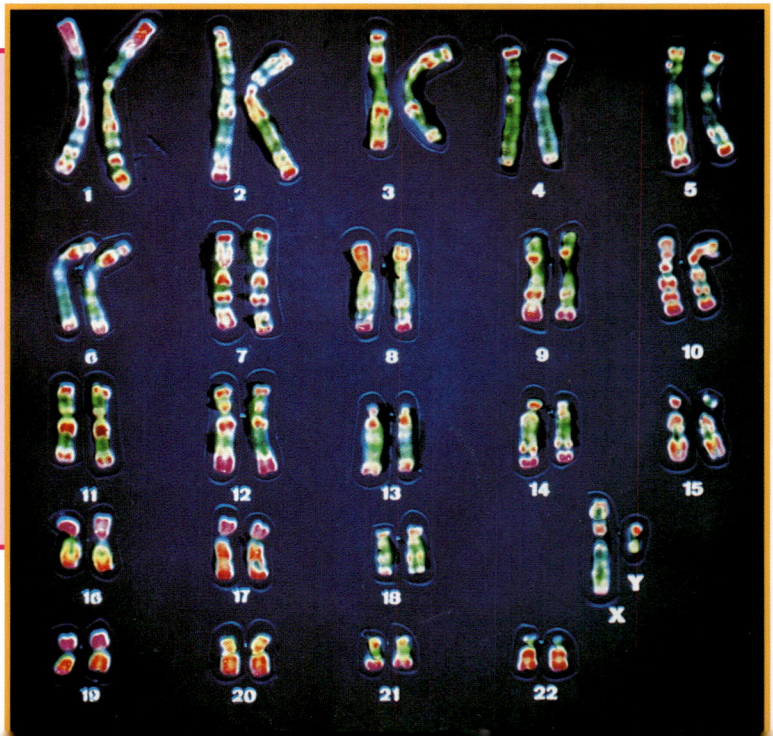

*If you have Down's syndrome, it is a part of who you are and you will have it all your life. Many people with Down's syndrome are very proud of who they are. They think others with the **condition** should feel the same as they do.*

What happens in Down's syndrome?

No one really knows for certain why or how it happens, but babies born with Down's syndrome have an extra chromosome. They have 47 chromosomes, not 46. It is nothing to do with something their parents did or did not do. It is simply that they are born with three number 21 chromosomes instead of two. The extra chromosome is present in every cell in their bodies.

This tiny difference is what causes Down's syndrome. The extra genes on this extra chromosome slightly alters the way a person develops. This is why Down's syndrome is not an illness or a disease. It is simply a part of who that person is. It is as much a part of them as the colour of their eyes or hair.

What is it like?

Everyone who has Down's syndrome is an individual.
People who have Down's syndrome vary enormously in
the way they look, the way they are and what they can
do, just like other people. Like everyone else, children
with Down's syndrome look more like their families
than they do anyone else. As individuals, they also have
their own features, the things that make them unique.

Physically, though, people with Down's syndrome tend
to be rather short in height. They may have quite a
stocky body, arms and legs. Many have a round face
with eyelids that slope upwards slightly. Not everyone
who has Down's syndrome has these features and, if they
do, they may have one or all of the features.

Although there may be some similarities between people who have Down's syndrome, individuals look much more like their brothers, sisters, mothers and fathers, than they do others with Down's syndrome.

Health

Some people who have Down's syndrome are fit and healthy, and do not have any more health problems than others of their age. Other people with Down's syndrome find that they are more prone to certain health problems than other people.

Lots of people wear glasses to help them see. Many young people with Down's syndrome have glasses, too.

Some people with Down's syndrome have problems with their hearing, their sight or both. Some have more **infections** than others of their age. For example, they may have respiratory infections (problems with breathing). It may also take them longer to get over these infections than other people. Some people with Down's syndrome have problems with their heart or **digestive system**, usually when they are very young. Today, most of these health problems can be cured or treated. People take medicines to treat their infections and they may be able to have operations to make their heart or digestive system better.

Early days

Anyone can be born with Down's syndrome. So how can doctors tell if someone has the **condition**? Doctors or nurses may suspect Down's syndrome because of the way a baby looks. For example, babies with Down's syndrome often have a single crease across the centre of the palm of their hands and they may weigh less than other babies. However, babies who do not have Down's syndrome may have these features, too. The only way to be certain a baby has Down's syndrome is to do a special test. A tiny sample of blood or skin is taken, and doctors test it to see if the **cells** contain an extra **chromosome**.

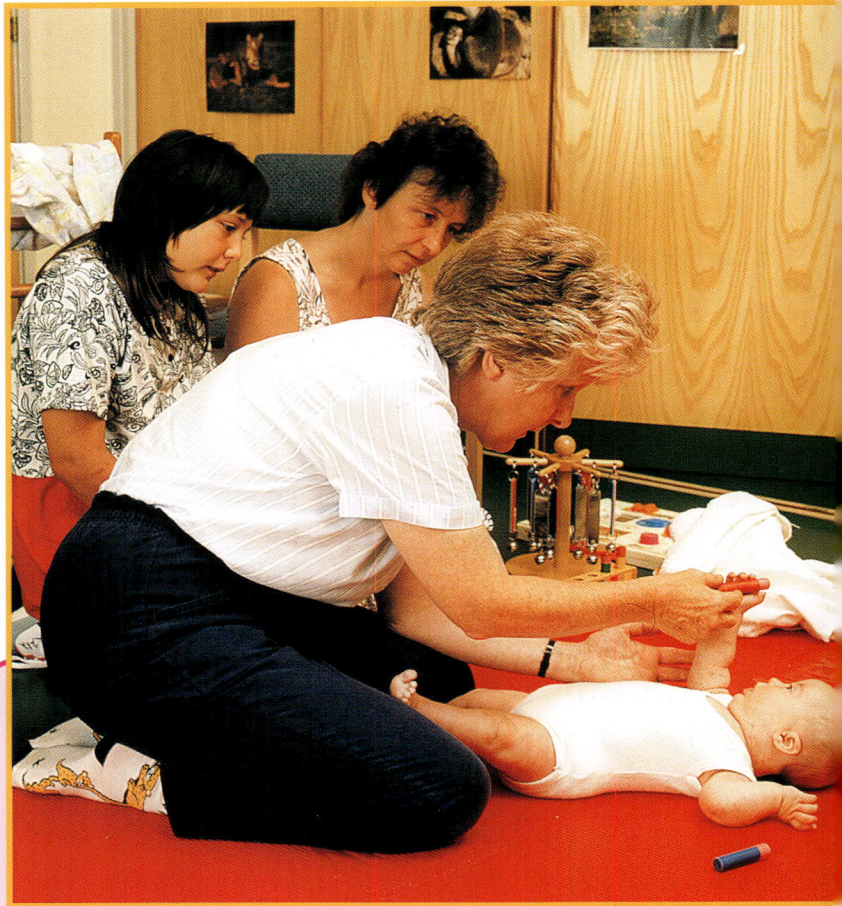

Most babies with Down's syndrome get lots of help to make sure they stay healthy and happy.

It is important to find out if a baby has Down's syndrome as early as possible. The sooner any problems with the heart or **digestive system** are discovered, the earlier they can be treated. This will give the child a healthier start in life.

First steps

All babies learn to do things in different ways and at slightly different times. Some babies crawl or shuffle on their bottoms long before they manage to walk. Other babies walk before they are even a year old. Babies who are born with Down's syndrome learn to do everything other babies do. It may just take them a little more time and they may need a little more help. Eventually, most young children who have Down's syndrome learn to sit, walk, talk and ride a bike, just like other young children.

Facts about Down's syndrome

- About one in every 800 to 1000 babies born has Down's syndrome.
- All children with Down's syndrome have difficulty learning. In some, it is a lot; in many, it is very little.
- Babies are born with Down's syndrome because they have an extra chromosome in the cells in their bodies.
- Down's syndrome is not caused by anything the parents did or did not do before their baby was born.

Almost all babies with Down's syndrome reach their first milestones, such as their first steps or their first words. They just reach them a bit later than other children.

Meet Karen and Kieran

Hello. I'm Karen and I'm Kieran's mum. Kieran is seven years old now. He's a very healthy, happy boy, but he hasn't always been like that. When he was born he was very blue. The doctors at our local hospital were very worried about his colour and sent us to another hospital so a **specialist** could see him. It turned out that Kieran had quite a serious heart problem, and one that was quite rare even in children with Down's syndrome. His heart was not pumping blood around his body efficiently, and your blood carries the **oxygen** (air) you need to live.

Kieran had an emergency operation when he was two weeks old to help him get the oxygen he needed. Then, when he was two years old, doctors fully repaired his heart. He has a check-up every year, just to make sure his heart is OK, but he doesn't need to take any medicines. He does tend to have lots of colds and coughs, which happens with some children who have Down's syndrome. But, on the whole, he is fit and well and can do whatever he likes.

Kieran goes to the local primary school. In the mornings, he and another girl with Down's syndrome have a support worker, called Chris, to help them. She helps them and other people in the class when they need it. Kieran works with Chris by himself sometimes, or she helps him in the classroom. In the afternoons, he has the same lessons as everyone else and the teacher makes sure the work he gets suits him. He is getting on very well with his reading. It took a while to learn because he recognizes whole words rather than individual letters, but he loves reading now. He wears glasses for reading, though his sight is fine otherwise.

Kieran likes everything at school except art and cooking. He hates getting his hands dirty! At nursery school, he hated the sandpit. At home, he likes watching videos. He also loves swimming – he goes once a week with his dad. He spends a lot of time playing with his sister, either indoors or in the garden. Another thing he loves is music. He learns the words to songs very quickly and sings along. He dances, too, and he's very good at interpreting the songs, matching his dance moves to the music.

Growing up with Down's syndrome

Each child who has Down's syndrome is different and as they grow up they may need different kinds of support. Some children with Down's syndrome have health problems which need treating. Others are perfectly healthy, but they may have difficulties learning. Sometimes problems with your health can affect how you learn. For example, it is important for children with Down's syndrome who have sight or hearing problems to get help for these because it is hard to learn to talk, read and write if you cannot see or hear properly.

When children who have Down's syndrome grow up there are all kinds of jobs they can do.

If you have Down's syndrome, the important thing is that you get whatever kind of help you need to make the best of your abilities. As they grow up, children who have Down's syndrome learn to take care of themselves and help around the house, just like everyone else. They have hobbies and interests, make friends and go to school. As adults, many people with Down's syndrome work in a whole range of jobs – in offices, banks, businesses or restaurants. They work with people, or using machines or computers.

Going to school

Some children who have Down's syndrome go to special schools, where all the teachers are trained to help children who need to learn in different ways. Here, children are taught in smaller groups. This makes it is easier for the teacher to give them help and to be sure that all the children understand what they are learning. Most young children with Down's syndrome go to ordinary schools and do the same lessons as their classmates. They usually have the help of an assistant teacher. This extra teacher gives them any help they need, but they work on their own as well.

If you have a friend in your class who has Down's syndrome, you may notice that they learn more slowly than others. We all learn at different speeds and find some subjects easier to understand than others. The important thing is that we learn new things and make progress ourselves, not in comparison with other people.

School is not just about learning English, maths and science. It is also a chance to work happily with lots of different people.

Keeping well

To keep fit and well, people with Down's syndrome need to do the same as anyone else. It is important for us all to eat a healthy diet. That means eating a range of foods, including a little **protein** and **fat** every day, lots of fruit and vegetables, and some **carbohydrates**, such as bread, cereals or pasta, at every meal. We should also try to drink plenty of water and take regular exercise. Doing these things makes us feel better and keeps us fitter. It also means that our bodies should be better able to fight off **infections**.

Most children also have **vaccinations**. Vaccinations are injections that help our bodies fight infections that could make us ill. Young people with Down's syndrome have the same vaccinations as anyone else. They may also have some extra ones as well, for example to reduce the chances of them catching influenza ('flu). It is also important for everyone to visit their doctor for regular health checks. That way, a doctor can spot a health problem before it becomes too serious.

If you have Down's syndrome you need to take care of yourself to keep well, just like anyone else. Most of the time, you can be as busy as you want to!

Hear this!

Hearing problems can affect anyone's ability to speak because they cannot hear how words are said properly. Many young children have hearing problems. In about one in four children this may be caused by 'glue ear'. Glue ear often happens when someone has an infection, such as a cold. A sticky fluid (the 'glue') blocks up a part of the ear, making it hard for sounds to get through. Usually, when the cold goes away the blockage does, too. If it does not, a doctor can put a tiny tube into the ear to drain off the fluid. Some children who have Down's syndrome get more ear infections than other children. This often means they are more likely to have speech or hearing problems caused by glue ear.

Speaking and listening

Some children who have Down's syndrome have difficulty speaking clearly. This is usually because the muscles in their mouth and tongue are a little slack (floppy), so it is hard for them to make the sounds clearly.

Speech and language therapists can help some people with Down's syndrome to speak more clearly.

Ways of learning

We all learn in different ways. Some of us find things easier to remember or understand if they are written down. Others find it easier to learn by doing things, such as science experiments, for themselves. People who have Down's syndrome usually have some kind of **learning difficulty**. Sometimes this is caused by a physical problem – if you find it hard to control a pen or a paintbrush, you may have difficulties writing or painting. Other people with Down's syndrome have trouble remembering too many things at once. They may find it easier to do schoolwork in smaller sections, or to have some extra time to think about what they have to do.

Many children who have Down's syndrome are very good at observing things in subjects such as science.

Many children with Down's syndrome are very good at learning from what they see and do. Because they have trouble remembering and thinking about too many things at once, it is often hard for them to learn from listening to the teacher for a long time. They may be much better at learning from what they can see, such as information in books.

Computers can be fun!

Many of us enjoy working on a computer. For children who learn most easily from what they can see and do, computers can be especially useful. Information on a computer is presented visually – that means you see it. As well as giving information and ideas in words on the screen, lots of computer programs today can show you things in pictures, cartoons or videos, usually with accompanying sound effects. Seeing and hearing the same information in many different forms is a great way of helping you to remember it.

Using a computer can help because programs often break work down into one task at a time. You can choose for yourself when you are ready to move on to the next step.

When you work on a computer, you are also in control of what you do. You can take as long as you like to finish working on something before moving on. You can easily go back over things you may have found hard to understand or remember. Computers can also be great fun. Many programs offer you rewards when you finish a piece of work, such as games or puzzles.

Meet Becky

Hello. My name is Becky. I am nine years old. I have a brother called Michael. He is six. I like playing with him. We like playing 'It'. We've got a slide in the garden and we like playing on that, too. I've got a cat. She is called Tiggy. She likes to eat a lot. She likes being cuddled as well. She sits on my lap. I help look after her and feed her. I also like to help Mum. I help unload the dishwasher and the washing machine, and I do other things as well, like tidy my room.

I like school a lot. I've got lots of friends at school. My best friend is called Chris. Writing is one of my favourite things. I've got writing homework to do tonight. I do my writing on a computer. I sit at the big table in the front room so I can watch the telly at the same time.

I go to a dance class every Friday after school. I do ballroom dancing and I do dancing to pop music as well. I've won six rosettes for my dancing. I like listening to pop music. I've got a radio in my room and I like watching *Top of the Pops* on TV after dance class. My favourite group is Steps. I've got a Steps CD and I play it a lot.

I also like swimming. We go to a pool up the road. I'm good at doing the crawl. And I like ten-pin bowling where you have to roll a ball and knock down pins. I go with my dad, my brother and my nanny. I'm good at it – even better than my dad!

Living with Down's syndrome

Many people with Down's syndrome are proud of who they are and they feel that everyone who has Down's syndrome should be proud of themselves, too. Most people who have Down's syndrome say that it is only a small part of their lives. They have lots of other things to do and to think about.

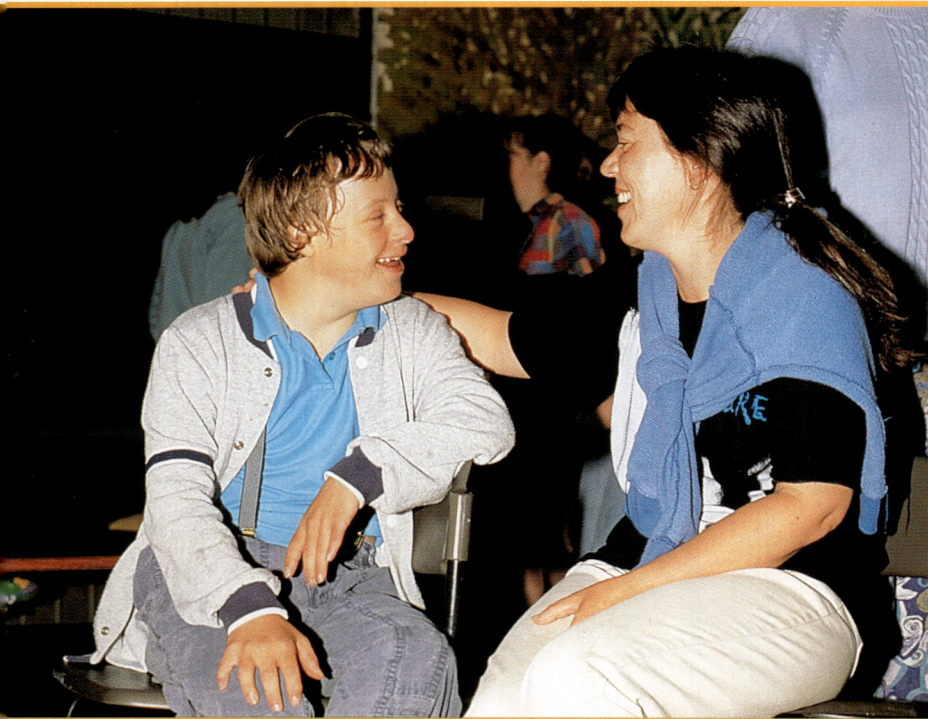

People with Down's syndrome don't feel sorry for themselves and they say there is no reason for other people to feel sorry for them either. They just want to get on with their lives, like everyone else.

Even so, people with Down's syndrome are just like everyone else, and they have times when they feel sad or unhappy. At times like these, they may do all sorts of different things to cheer themselves up. Some people make themselves a plate of their favourite food. Other people do something active that they are really good at, such as swimming, to make themselves feel better. Sometimes talking to your family and friends can help. What do you do to cheer yourself up when you feel sad?

Other people

Many children with Down's syndrome say that they are bullied at times. They may be called names, stared at or even pushed around. If you or someone you know has ever been bullied, you will know just how hurtful it can be. Children with Down's syndrome are just like everyone else – their feelings can be badly hurt, too.

Bullying sometimes happens because people don't understand what Down's syndrome is. They may resort to teasing because they don't know what else to say to someone who has Down's syndrome. Some children have found that it helps to be brave and talk about the bullying. They, a parent or a teacher, give a talk to their class to explain what Down's syndrome is and how much it hurts to be laughed at. This helps other people to understand that they are just like anyone else; they just have a few extra problems to deal with.

*If you have Down's syndrome, it can help if classmates understand what the **condition** means for you. This should help them to understand if, for example, it takes you a bit longer to learn the rules of a playground game.*

At school

Many children who have Down's syndrome go to ordinary schools. They usually do the same lessons and activities as other children their age. Because they have some difficulties learning, there will usually be a learning assistant in class who can help them out when they need it. This assistant sits in on lessons and helps the person with Down's syndrome and the other pupils in the class if they get stuck.

If you have Down's syndrome, having help in class gives you a chance to do the best work that you can.

Learning assistants help in all sorts of ways. For example, if you have Down's syndrome, you may find it difficult to follow a long list of instructions, say for a project. The assistant might be able to help by explaining what you have to do in a different way, or by helping you to break the work down into smaller, more manageable bits. Some children who have Down's syndrome may need quite a lot of assistance from their classroom helper; others may be able to manage by themselves for most of the time.

Exercise is good for you!

Exercise is good for everyone and most children with Down's syndrome take part in school sports activities, just like everyone else. Some children with Down's syndrome may have more difficulties with things such as skipping, running, throwing and catching. This is because their muscles may be a bit slacker (looser) than other people's, so they don't have such easy control over them. They usually find another form of sport or exercise that they enjoy and are good at, such as skating or swimming.

Some people with Down's syndrome get very hot or very cold easily. Others may have a **condition**, such as a heart problem, which means they soon get tired. At times like these, they may have to take time out to rest. If you have any of these problems, you usually know yourself when you need to sit out for a while and when you feel fit enough to join in again.

We should all do some exercise or sport to keep us fit and healthy. Children with Down's syndrome enjoy many different kinds of sport, from skateboarding and swimming to skiing and dancing!

At home

Children with Down's syndrome make friends at school and at home, just like anyone else. Most of these friends probably won't have Down's syndrome.

What is life at home like for people who have Down's syndrome? Well, the answer is pretty much the same as it is for anyone else! Home is where we can relax and do the things that we enjoy. Most children who have Down's syndrome live at home with their families. They play with their brothers and sisters, or friends who live nearby. They have as wide a range of interests as anyone else. They take part in local clubs and events, playing sports or music, as well as doing any other hobbies they enjoy.

Making friends

Some people also like to spend some time at clubs or groups especially for young people with **learning difficulties**. They may enjoy meeting other people who share some of the same experiences as them. It can be good to meet other young people who know how it feels to have Down's syndrome. Of course, they mostly go to clubs and groups like this to have fun!

Brothers and sisters

What about the brothers or sisters of someone who has Down's syndrome? Most people say that they get on very well with their brother or sister who has Down's syndrome. They are very fond of them. They spend lots of time playing games or enjoying other things, such as music or reading, together.

Some people find that having a brother or sister who has extra difficulties can be hard at times. It may seem as if they get more attention because they need extra help sometimes, perhaps with schoolwork. If someone is rude or inconsiderate to their brother or sister, they may feel angry or embarrassed. However, most children who have a brother or sister with Down's syndrome say that if it has made a difference to their lives, it is for the better. They feel that they are more mature and understanding about other people they meet who have learning or physical difficulties than most other children their age.

Everyone has times when they get fed up with their brothers and sisters. That is only natural. Most of the time, though, it is impossible to imagine life without them!

Meet Katherine

My name is Isabel and my daughter Katherine has Down's syndrome. Katherine is thirteen years old and goes to the local secondary school, which she loves. She has lots of friends there. She does gym classes, an Animal Action class, in which she does projects about animals, such as making bird tables, as well as the usual classes.

I drop Katherine off at school in the mornings or she goes on the bus with an older school friend. She can find her way around school perfectly well on her own. In classes, Katherine has a morning and an afternoon helper. They help her take part in school lessons. For instance, they help her take notes because she writes more slowly and needs help with spellings. Otherwise, she does the same work, just at a slightly simpler level. The helpers don't go with her for gym or PE. She enjoys gym very much and was in the annual gym display at the school last year.

Katherine does a dance class every week with other children who have Down's syndrome. Most of the time she does things with her friends from school, including Guides, swimming and a club at the local church.

Katherine enjoys working with her classroom helper.

My name is Katherine. I live with my mum and dad, my brothers Edward and William, and my sister Elizabeth. At school, I like drama. I like acting out. We do role-play. We did one about the railway. I was a passenger. I like Chemistry, too. I got a high score in my test. I like practical work and experiments. I've got lots of friends. I like listening to music with them. We eat lunch together. I see them at Guides, too.

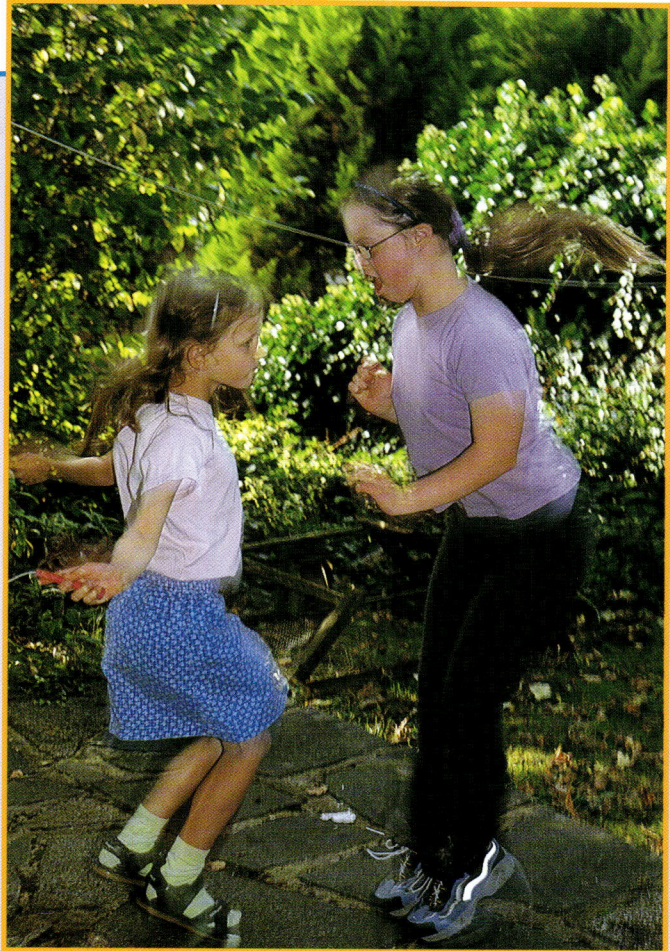

When I'm not at school I go to Guides. We play games, stay up late, sometimes we go swimming and sometimes we go out for a burger, we cook and we make things. I listen to pop music on my CD player. I go to church. I play the keyboard. I like drawing and blending pastel colours together. I look after my guinea pig called Lucy. I do gym club and dance class. Angelina teaches us dance. All the people there have Down's syndrome. It is good. I have Down's syndrome. Down's syndrome makes my friends look after me. Mrs Westall helps me in school. I am like my friends but I am special.

Glossary

carbohydrates nutrients from some of the foods we eat. Carbohydrates give us energy.

cells tiny living 'building blocks' that make up all the different parts of your body. You can see cells only with a powerful microscope. There are many different kinds of cells, in different shapes and sizes, depending on the job they do in the body.

chromosomes tiny, thread-like structures found inside cells. They carry genes – the information for all the characteristics, such as colour of eyes or hair, which we inherit (get) from our parents.

condition physical complaint that is not a disease or an illness

digestive system parts of the body, including your stomach and intestines, which help you digest your food

fat nutrient found in some foods, like butter. It is not healthy to eat or drink too much fat.

genes things that determine how we look and what we are like, such as whether we are tall or short, or what colour our hair and eyes are

infection kind of disease that can be caught from other people. The most common infectious disease is the cold.

learning difficulties when someone has a condition, such as Down's syndrome, which means that they find it harder to learn things

oxygen type of gas in the air that we breathe. We need oxygen because it helps our bodies to turn the food we eat into energy. We need energy for everything we do – to live, move and grow.

ovum egg cell from the mother, which joins with the sperm cell from the father to start a baby growing inside the mother

protein nutrient found in food such as eggs, cheese, nuts and meat. Protein helps our bodies grow and repair themselves.

specialist someone who has a lot of training and experience in a particular subject

speech and language therapist person who advises and helps people who have problems with speaking and listening

sperm cell from the father, which joins with the ovum (egg cell) from the mother to start a baby growing inside the mother

symptom something that your body feels that tells us something is wrong and that you have a disease or condition

vaccination injection of a vaccine. A vaccine is a safe amount of the germs of a particular disease. This helps your body to recognize and kill off any further germs of the disease that enter your body.

Helpful books and addresses

BOOKS
Living With Down's Syndrome, Jenny Bryan, Hodder Wayland, 2000
I Know How My Cells Make Me Grow, Walker Books, 2000

ORGANIZATIONS
The Down's Syndrome Association is a charity that works with people who have Down's syndrome. It provides support, information and advice to people with Down's syndrome, their parents, families and carers.
155 Mitcham Road
London SW17 9PG
Tel: 0208 682 4001
Fax: 0208 682 4012
Website: www.downs-syndrome.org.uk

IN AUSTRALIA
(Note that in Australia people say 'Down syndrome')

Down Syndrome Association of Queensland
PO Box 3223
Stafford, QLD, 4053
Telephone: 07 3356 6655
Fax: 07 3856 2687
Website: www.uq.net.au

Down Syndrome Society of South Australia
24 Harrow Avenue
Magill SA 5072
Telephone: 08 8365 3510
Fax: 08 8365 0170
Website: www.downssa.mtx.net

Down Syndrome Association of NSW Inc
31 O'Connell Street
Parramatta NSW 2150
PO Box 2356
North Parramatta NSW 1750
Telephone: 02 9683 4333
Fax: 02 9683 4020
Website: www.dsansw@hartingdale.com.au

Index